Rain Forests

Steve Parker

QEB Publishing

QEB

Copyright © QEB Publishing, Inc. 2008

Published in the United States by
QEB Publishing, Inc.
3 Wrigley, Suite A
Laguna Hills, CA 92618

www.qeb-publishing.com

Library of Congress Cataloging-in-Publication Data

Parker, Steve.
  Rainforests / Steve Parker.
      p. cm. -- (Planet earth)
  Includes index.
  Summary: "Describes the climate, locations, types,
and plants and animals of rainforest ecosystems"--
Provided by publisher.
  ISBN 978-1-59566-571-3
  1. Rain forest ecology--Juvenile literature. 2. Rain
forests--Juvenile literature. I. Title.
  QH541.5.R27.P37 2009
  577.34--dc22
                                    2008012592

ISBN 978 1 59566 969 8

Printed and bound in China

Author Steve Parker
Design and Editorial East River Partnership

Publisher Steve Evans
Creative Director Zeta Davies

Picture credits
(t = top, b = bottom, l = left, r = right,
c = center, FC = front cover)
Getty Images 4–5b Mattius Klum/National,
Geographic, 5b Maria Stenzel, 8 Tom Till,
10 Gerry Ellis, 13 Pete Oxford, 14t Timothy Laman,
16–17 Norbert Wu, 19b DEA/R Sacco, 20 Art
Wolfe, 25 Tui De Roy

NHPA 12t Nick Garbutt, 14 Stephen Dalton, 15r,
23t, 28–29b Martin Harvey, 18–19t John Shaw,
27 Nigel J Dennis, 28–29t Martin Wendler

Shutterstock 1, 2, 3, 30, 31, 32 Dr Morley Read, 1
Eric Isselee, 1 Mark Grenier, 1, 8b John Bell,
3, 16t Snowleopard1, 4–5t Joe Gough,
5t EcoPrint, 7t Jennifer Stone, 8b Olga Shelego,
9 Suzanne Long, 11t Leo, 12b jaana piira,
16b Luis Louro, 17t Timothy Craig Lubcke,
18–19b Sergey I, 19t chai kian shin,
20b Michael Shake, 21t Karel Gallas,
21 Alvaro Pantoja, 22l Peter Graham,
22t Vova Pomortzeff, 22 Galyna Andrushko,
24 Donald Gargano, 25b fenghui,
26 Jim Lipschutz, 27 Patsy A Jacks,
28l Simone van den Berg, 29r Grigory Kubatyan,
31 szefei

Words in bold are
explained in the glossary
on page 30.

Contents

Rain and forest

Rain forests are well named. They have lots of tall trees, close together, and it rains and rains and rains!

Warm and wet

Rain forests are wet nearly all year round. Although there may be a short dry season lasting a few weeks, it rains almost every day, week after week. **Tropical** rain forests are not only wet, they are also very warm. The temperature is at least 68°F on most days, and sometimes higher than 86°F.

Rain forest trees grow close together, forming a thick, green covering.

The rare Asiatic lion now lives only in India's Gir rain forest.

Wow!

Although rain forests cover only one-sixteenth of the Earth's land area, they are home to more than half of all animals, plants, and other living things.

Mangrove trees grow along some tropical coasts.

Plants and animals

Living things grow fast in a tropical rain forest's damp, steamy warmth. There are lots of amazing plants, from tiny flowers to enormous trees. Animals of every kind also live here, including worms and bugs, colorful frogs, screeching birds, huge elephants, leaping monkeys, and shy gorillas.

It's so... wet!

Some rain forests get more than five times the rain in New York City, eight times more rain than London, and fifteen times more than Los Angeles.

Rain forest people get food from plants in the forest.

Types of rain forest

Rain forests grow mainly around the middle of the world, on either side of the equator. This area is called the tropics, where it is warm all year.

NORTH AMERICA

Central America

Amazon

SOUTH AMERICA

Water vapor

As winds blow over oceans, they take up water. Winds do not carry water as a liquid, but as **vapor** that floats in the air and cannot be seen. The vapor makes the winds feel damp. When these winds blow over land, the water vapor changes into drops of water. These clump together to form clouds and fall as rain. Rain forests grow where there is most rain.

Wow!

Each year, it rains on about 120 days in New York City, 180 days in London and more than 300 days in some rain forests.

It's so... cool!

The average temperature in rain forests in the south of New Zealand's South Island is just 48°F. Some tropical rain forests are three times hotter than this.

Clouds blowing in from the sea keep rain forests wet and steamy.

■ Temperate rain forests
■ Tropical rain forests

Japan

South-east Asia

The biggest rain forest areas are in South America, Africa, and South-east Asia.

Philippines

Sumatra

Borneo

EQUATOR

New Guinea

Java

Warm and cool

Tropical rain forests near the **equator** are warm all year, and have the most plants and animals. There are **temperate** rain forests in cooler places, such as along the western coast of North America and on the island of Tasmania.

Madagascar

Australia

New Zealand

7

Layers of the rain forest

From the ground to the treetops, a rain forest has different layers where all sorts of animals and plants live.

Dim and quiet

If you walk though a rain forest, you notice that the forest floor is a dim and quiet place. Few flowers grow, and most animals that live here hide away. Not far above are the tops of tall bushes, shrubs, and young trees. This is the understory layer.

It's so... scary!

The world's biggest spider lives on the rain forest floor in South America. The goliath tarantula is too big to sit on a dinner plate!

Wow!

Busy and noisy

The **canopy layer** of a rain forest is a tangle of branches, twigs, leaves, flowers, and fruits. It is a busy and noisy place, as most rain forest animals live here. Further up, there are taller trees. These form the **emergent layer**, where monkeys and eagles look across the rain forest.

Rain forests are split into four different layers.

Emergent layer

Canopy layer

Understory layer

Forest floor

Rain forest animals

Rain forests are full of creatures, many of which hide away and are difficult to find.

Slimy trails

Rain forests are home to many types of animal. Most common are small insects, such as flies, ants, and termites. Brightly colored butterflies fly between flowers, and snails and slugs leave slimy trails.

Spider monkeys feast on fruits and flowers.

Swinging monkeys

The agile spider monkey, which lives in South American rain forests, swings from tree to tree using its hands, feet, and tail to grab and hold branches. Below, fish and turtles swim in pools and swamps.

It's so huge!

The world's biggest snakes live in rain forests. In Africa and Asia, enormous pythons swallow **prey** that is sometimes the size of a pig!

The jaguar's spotted coat helps it to hide in the shadows of the forest.

Toucans crack nuts with their huge bill.

Screeching toucans

Rain forests are also home to cats of all sizes. The marbled cat of Asia looks like a tiny leopard, while the jaguar of South America is almost as big as a lion. In the trees, parrots, macaws, and toucans screech and flap between the branches.

Wow!

The biggest tree-dwelling animal is the orangutan of South-east Asia. A fully grown male can weigh 176 pounds—as much as a person.

Male crickets chirp
to attract females.

Sounds of the rain forest

The rain forest can be one of the noisiest places in the natural world, especially at dawn and dusk.

Howler monkeys roar to protect their territory.

Day and night

Sometimes the rain forest is quiet. In the middle of the day, and for most of the night, many animals rest. At dawn and **dusk**, it is very different. Gibbons whoop, monkeys holler, birds chirrup, frogs croak, crickets and cicadas chirp, and flies and bees buzz.

Hyacinth macaws squawk warnings to other members of their flock.

The loudest animal for its size is the cicada. If this insect was as big as a person, its chirps would be heard 12 miles away!

Wow!

It's so... loud!

The world's loudest land animals are South American howler monkeys. Their whoops carry for 3 miles through the treetops.

Attracting partners

Many of the larger creatures make sounds to defend their territory. This is the area of forest where they live and feed. Their calls warn others to stay away. Some animals, such as frogs, crickets, and birds, make special songs and sounds at breeding time to attract partners.

Colugos use skin flaps to glide from tree to tree.

Moving through the trees

Most rain forest animals live in the branches of the rain forest canopy. They have different ways of moving around the trees.

Twisting and turning

Flying is a great way to travel through, and over, the rain forest. Eagles soar above the canopy looking for prey, such as monkeys and sloths. Hawks twist and turn among the branches to grab smaller birds. At night, bats snap up insects and owls swoop down on mice and lizards.

Some flying lizards can glide up to 328 feet, using their tail to steer.

Fastest mover

One of the fastest rain forest movers is the gibbon. It swings from tree to tree using its long, powerful arms, hanging by its hook-like hands.

Gliding around

Some rain forest animals that seem to fly are really gliding through the air. Flying lizards, flying squirrels, flying frogs, and flying snakes all use large flaps of parachute-like body skin to glide around.

Gibbons have curved hands and feet to grip branches.

It's so... small!

The world's smallest mammal is the bumblebee bat of South-east Asia. With a body as small as a bumblebee, this tiny bat weighs less than a US 5cent coin.

Wow!

The best glider is the flying lemur, or colugo, of South-east Asia. It is not a true flier, nor a lemur, but it can glide for more than 492 feet.

Deadly killers

Rain forest creatures are always on the lookout for danger. There could be a killer on the next branch!

Deadly poisons

Not all killers are big. Many rain forest spiders, centipedes, and scorpions use poisonous bites or stings to kill their prey. Some tiny South American frogs have deadly poisons in their skin, and bright colors to warn other creatures not to eat them! Local people tip their blowdarts, arrows, and spears with this poison.

The poison from one bite of a king cobra can kill an elephant.

Tiny poison arrow frogs are only as long as your thumb.

Wow!

The poison in the skin of one poison arrow frog is so powerful it could kill up to 20 people!

Large predators

Some of the world's most powerful **predators** live in rain forests. The largest big cat is the tiger, which stalks Asian rain forests for deer and wild pigs. In South America, the caiman lurks near swamps and snaps up turtles and fish. Growing up to 551 pounds, the Amazon's green anaconda is the world's heaviest snake.

Tigers are the largest hunters in the rain forest.

Caimans catch fish, turtles, and crabs.

It's so... poisonous!

The king cobra of Asia is the world's longest poisonous snake. It grows to be more than 16 feet long, and its favorite food is other snakes!

Rain forest trees

Some of the world's tallest, heaviest, and fastest-growing trees are found in rain forests.

Life in a tree

Thousands of creatures depend on a rain forest tree. Caterpillars munch its leaves, hummingbirds sip nectar from its flowers, monkeys eat its fruits, and birds nest in holes in its trunk. There are teak trees in Asia, mahogany trees in Africa and Central America, and rosewood trees around the world. The kapok tree of Central and South America grows to be 230 feet tall. That is the same height as an 18-story building.

Emerald tree boas wrap themselves around branches and wait for prey.

Insects that slip into a pitcher plant are digested.

Using camouflage

Some animals depend so much on trees, they look like them! Stick insects, or "walking sticks," resemble twigs. Leaf insects and the tree boa snake are green, just like leaves. The colorful flower mantis is disguised as a flower. Looking like part of the surroundings to avoid being seen is called **camouflage**.

Rosewood trees are under threat from loggers, who cut them for their sweet-smelling wood.

Wow!

A few rain forest flowers grow high above the forest floor, sometimes 164 feet up in the forks of great trees.

Cooktown orchids grow in rain forests in north-eastern Australia.

The teeming canopy

In the rain forest canopy, twigs, stems, buds, blossom, fruits, and seeds provide food for a huge variety of animals.

Bird life

Colorful small birds, such as sunbirds, honeyeaters, and motmots, fly among branches in the rain forest. The great hornbill of South Asia has a wingspan of 5 feet and a huge **casque** on its head. The world's biggest eagles, the harpy eagle of Central and South America and the Philippine eagle, prey on monkeys, sloths, snakes, and birds.

The great hornbill digs out insects from trees with its powerful beak.

Morpho butterflies find sunny clearings to warm themselves.

Pygmy marmosets live on the sap of rain forest trees.

Sloths sleep for 16 hours each day.

Hanging around

Some animals that live in the canopy never come down to the ground. These include monkeys, tree rats, and lizards, such as iguanas and geckos. One of the slowest creatures in the canopy is the sloth. This leaf eater hangs from branches by its long curved claws, sometimes spending an entire week feeding on one tree.

It's so... little!

Marmosets are little South American rain forest monkeys. The smallest is the pygmy marmoset, with a head and body as small as a human fist.

The rafflesia plant has no leaves.

The forest floor

Some of the world's biggest and most exciting animals slip through the shadows of the rain forest floor.

Forest elephants live in small groups.

The forest okapi is a relative of the giraffe.

Moving silently

Elephants may seem easy to spot but, in West Africa, forest elephants move almost silently among the trees, hardly noticed in the gloom. Lowland gorillas, the world's biggest apes, also live here. These gentle creatures eat leaves and fruits. Tapirs are pig-like animals with a long, bendy nose. They live in South American and Asian rain forests.

The tapir's fleshy nose helps it to grab soft, tasty leaves.

WOW!

The capybara, a huge cousin of the guinea pig, lives in South American rain forests. Weighing more than 132 pounds, it is the world's largest rodent.

Darkness below

The floor of the rain forest gets little light because of the thick canopy high above. Few small plants are able to survive on the ground. Only when a huge tree has fallen down will sunlight break through. Then the seeds of flowers, bushes, and trees can grow.

It's so... smelly!

At 3 feet wide, the rafflesia of South-east Asia is the world's largest flower. It attracts flies to carry its **pollen** by smelling of rotting meat!

Mountain forests

Not all rain forests are found on flat lowlands. Some have developed on the sides of steep hills and mountains.

Furry gorillas

Tropical mountain rain forests grow high up. In these regions, it is not only very wet, but also cooler than in tropical lowlands. Here, animals have thick fur to keep warm. The furry mountain gorillas that live in Central Africa sleep in trees at night. Mother gorillas bend branches together to make a nest for themselves and their babies. Big male gorillas, which can weigh more than 440 pounds, sleep in grassy nests on the ground.

A big male gorilla, or silverback, will protect his family group.

It's so... rare!

With just a few hundred left, the mountain gorilla is one of the world's rarest big animals.

Bamboo eater

The spectacled bear of South America lives in rain forests that are 1.5 miles high in the Andes mountains. This bear eats almost any food, plant, or animal. The giant panda from the cool, damp, cloudy hills of south-east China, however, prefers to eat just one kind of food. It rarely eats anything other than bamboo.

Wow!

A fully grown giant panda is bigger than a person. A newborn giant panda, however, is tiny. It weighs about 3.5 ounces—less than an apple.

Spectacled bears can sniff out food hidden in the canopy.

Pandas have strong teeth to bite through bamboo.

Cool rain forests

Not all of the world's rain forests are warm and wet. Many are cool and wet, and are home for an amazing range of plants and animals.

Tallest trees

Rain forests in cooler regions are known as temperate rain forests. Although cool, these forests teem with life. They have the world's tallest trees, such as redwoods in America and kauri pines in New Zealand. These trees are called **evergreens**. This means that they keep their leaves all year, and their seeds grow in **cones**.

Many cooler rain forests grow on hills and mountains.

Wow!

The kakapo is a large New Zealand parrot. It cannot fly, it feeds at night, and there are fewer than 90 left alive. Scientists have given each one a name.

Birds and beavers

The floor of a temperate forest is wet and is covered with ferns, mosses, and creepers. Strange animals live in these cool rain forests, including the flightless kiwi bird of New Zealand and the mountain beaver of North America.

It's so... tall!

Cool rain forests have some of the tallest trees in the world. North American redwoods, Tasmanian giant gum trees and New Zealand kahikateas, or white pines, reach more than 230 feet in height.

The Tasmanian devil hunts for food at dusk in the rain forest.

The blue duiker is 12 inches tall—the same as a small dog.

Duikers and devils

The blue duiker is a small, shy antelope that lives in the cool forests of central and southern Africa. The stocky Tasmanian devil is an aggressive and noisy forest creature that has one of the most powerful bites of all mammals.

Disappearing rain forests

Rain forests are the richest places in the world for wildlife. But they are also places that are most at risk, and are disappearing fast.

Orangutans may be extinct in 30 years.

Laws against illegal logging are often ignored.

Destroying trees

Rain forests face many dangers, especially in the tropics. Here, trees are cut down for their strong timber, which is known as hardwood. With no trees left, many forest animals then have no homes. With no tree roots, forest soil gets washed away by heavy rain and blocks nearby rivers.

Cleared for crops

Rain forests are being cleared by fire to grow farm crops, such as sugar cane and oil palm trees. Many areas are also being planted with grass to feed cows and other **livestock**. Some rain forest animals are in danger because they are hunted for their meat.

Once the forest has been cleared, the land is used to grow crops.

There are only about 60 Javan rhinos left in the rain forests of Java, Indonesia. It is doubtful that this rhino can survive.

Saving rain forests

All kinds of rain forest animals are at great risk, from butterflies and beetles to tigers, gorillas, and rhinos. We must work hard to save rain forests, with their wonderful plants and amazing creatures.

WOW!

An area of rain forest the size of a soccer pitch is cut down every second.

The Javan rhino is almost extinct in the wild.

Glossary

Camouflage Colors and patterns that blend with the surroundings, making a creature hard to see.

Canopy layer The main level of branches, leaves, and flowers in a rain forest, high above the ground.

Casque A helmet-like head covering.

Cone Hard, woody parts made by trees, such as pines and firs, which contain seeds.

Dusk The time around sunset, between day and night.

Emergent layer The tallest trees in a forest, above the main canopy layer.

Equator An imaginary line around the middle of the world, midway between the North Pole and South Pole.

Evergreen Trees that have some leaves all through the year.

Livestock Animals kept by people, especially on farms, such as cows, sheep, and pigs.

Pollen Tiny, dust-like grains that must get from the male parts of a flower to the female parts so that seeds can start to form.

Predator An animal that hunts others for food.

Prey An animal that is hunted for food.

Temperate Places where it is neither very hot nor very cold, usually with warm summers and cool winters.

Territory An area where an animal lives, feeds, and raises young, which it defends against others of its kind.

Tropical Around the middle of the world, in the region called the tropics, where it is very warm all year.

Understory layer Bushes, shrubs, young trees, and other low-growing plants in a forest.

Vapor Visible form of moisture floating in the air. Fog and steam are vapors.

Index